Totally Cute Kittens

This book belongs to...

Ticktock

An Hachette UK Company
www.hachette.co.uk

First published in the USA in 2015 by Ticktock.
an imprint of Octopus Publishing Group Ltd
Carmelite House, 50 Victoria Embankment
London, EC4Y 0DZ
www.octopusbooks.co.uk   www.octopusbooksusa.com   www.ticktockbooks.com
Copyright © Octopus Publishing Group Ltd 2015

Distributed in the US by
Hachette Book Group USA
1290 Avenue of the Americas
4th and 5th Floors
New York, NY 10020

Distributed in Canada by
Canadian Manda Group
664 Annette Street
Toronto, Ontario, Canada M6S 2C8

ISBN 978 1 78325 223 7
Printed and bound in China
10 9 8 7 6 5 4 3 2 1

Written by Mandy Archer
Designed by Doch & Doris Design and Development Ltd
Art Director: Miranda Snow
Managing Editor: Karen Rigden
Production Controller: Sarah-Jayne Johnson
US Editor: Jennifer Dixon

Picture Credits

Every effort has been made to trace the copyright holders, and we apologize in advance for any unintentional omissions. We would be pleased to insert the appropriate acknowledgement in any subsequent edition of this publication.

istockphoto.com   angusforbes 13 cr; Astakhova 26 ar; ChrisAt 23 bl; Eurngkwan 9 bl; GlobalP 17 bc, 49 bl; kot2626 28 br; Stefan-Weidner-Fotografie 23 al

Shutterstock   26kot 22 c; absolutimages 17 ac, 48 cl, 68 al, 70 main; Africa Studio 6 cl, 52 bl, 54 cr; anjoirina 52 ar; Al Nemer Olena 33a; Alena Ozerova 7 bcl, 12 ar, 13 ar, 67 bc; Alena Stalmashonak 79 al; Alexey Losevich 6 ar; Alta Oosthuizen 15 c; Anan Kaewkhammul 68 ar; Anastasija Popova 13 ar; Andrey_Kuzmin 13 bcr, 16 bl, 22 cl, 40 bl & br, 47 ar, 48 al; Anjalva 23 r; Anna Lisovskaya 67 ac; Anneka 51 main; Avesun 45 cl; Anthony Jay D Villalon 8 ar; Artem Kursin 29 br; Artem Zamula 77 br; BasPhoto 56 ar; berna namoglu 13 acl; Cherry-Merry 29 ar; Cindi Wilson 69 ac; Csaba Vanyi 41 cl; David Evison 7 bl; dien 10 bc, 11 cl; Elena Butinova 4 ar, 40 cl; Ermolaev Alexander 20 bl, 38 al, 41 cr & bl, 44 al, 49 al; Eric Isselée 16 br, 20 l, 36 ar, 53 al; ESOlex 32 a, 69 c; Eva Vargyasi 18 ar; Ewa Studio 55 cr; Flower_Power 66 bc; Foonia 22 cr; FotoYakov 52 cl; Gelpi JM 28 ar; Gladkova Svetlana 19 r, 55 bl, 80 br; GrigoryL 76 l; hannadarzy 78 al; hwongcc 16 c; Ilyashen-ko Oleksiy 7 main; ingret 68 bc; Inna Astakhova 17 ac, 44 br; IrinaK 48 bl; Jagodka 20 r, 55 br; Jesus Souto 11 cr; Kalmatsuy 63 cr; Katho Menden 8 bl; Komar 12 cl; Lana Langlois 4 c; Lars Christensen 53 ar; Leoba 21 c, 40 al; Liliya Kulianionak 45 cr; Linn Currie 3 b, 25 c, 35 main, 53 c, 71 main; Liudmila P. Sundikova 13 bl; Lubava 29 bc, 77 ar; makar 75 bc; MaraZe 12 al; Michal Dzierzynski 28 bl; Miles Away Photography 9 al; MustafaNC 38 ar; Nadinelle 66 br; Natalia7 38 br; NatUlrich 7 al; nelik 67 bl; Nikita Starichenko 9 br; Nina Buday 79 br; Oksana Kuzmina 13 br, 18 br; Olaf Speier 61 br; otsphoto 12 br; Paisit Teeraphatsakool 22 br; Pattakorn Uttarasak 38 bl; PixDeluxe 54 bl; Politchka 1 c; Poprotskiy Alexey 28 al; Renata Osinska 60 br; Rita Kochmarjova 66 ar, 78bl; s7chvetik 78 ar; Shvaygert Ekaterina 9 ar; Robynrg 6 br, 29 ac, 40 ar, 41 al; Sarah Fields Photography 57 br; Sarah Newton 24 c; schafar 67 ar; Scorpp 10 ac; Sinelyov 27 ar, 45 al; Sorina Madalina Androne 13 bl; Stefan Petru Andronache 54 al; tankist276 42 main; Termit 61 cl; tobkatrina 37 br; Tony Campbell 22 br, 37 al & bl, 53 bl, 68 br, 69 bl & br, 77 bc; Utekhina Anna 40 br; Vesna Cvorovic 36a; Victorian Traditions 7 bc; Vinogradov Illya 12 bl; Vitaliy Krasovskiy 55 al, 76 l; Vitaliya 5 c; Vitaly Titov & Maria Sidelnikova 76 r; vlada88 60 cr; vvita 58 & 59 main, 67 al; Zaretska Olga 46 main

Thinkstock   Anatolii Tsekhmister 30 r; Astakhova 26 cl, 36 cl; bulentozber 14 c; Carosch 66 ac; David De Lossy 66 bl; EEl_Tony 45 bc, 77 ac; Floriano Rescigno 56 bl; fotoedu 27 bc; GlobalP 29 al, 39 cr, 45 ar, 53 ac; heatheralvis 39 ar; icon72 57 cl; Ira Bachinskaya 44 ar; Katrina Brown 63 bc; Lars Christensen 36 br; Martin Poole 29 bl, 34 main, 50 main; nelik 44 bl; Okssi68 78 br; Olga Miltsova 52 ac; peplow 18 cl, 33 b; Philip Barlow 79 br; Svetlana Gladkova 31 bc; tobkatrina 61 cl; Tony Campbell 49 cl; Tsekhmister 30 l, 31 l & ar; vvita 66 al, 67 br; y_bashar_babur 79 bl; Yun Zhuo Zhang 57 ar.

Totally Cute Kittens

Contents

Too Cute!

Hi. Wanna play?

CHAPTER 1

Cat Crazy

Are you crazy for cats? Whether it's the cute fluffball that leaps out to pounce on your toes or the gorgeous kitty curled up asleep in the sunshine, every single one is a superstar! Playful, sweet, and fabulously furry, they're purr-fectly adorable!

Purr-fect Pets

Why are cats so fur-bulous?

Here are the top ten reasons why kitties are Very Important Pets!

1 There are millions of cats, but every single one is different. The nose pad on every kitty is unique, a bit like a human's fingerprint.

2 Cats are free spirits. They don't follow rules or routines - they come and go as they please!

3 They fall asleep in the funniest places. Bookshelves, handbags, and closets - kittens don't care! The average cat sleeps for at least 16 hours a day.

Cats like to look good, 24/7. After eating, even the youngest of kittens will stop to lick its paws clean.

5 They can see in the dark (almost).

6

There are all sorts of amazing breeds of cat, each with its own gorgeous look. Persian, Siamese, or Bengal - what's your favorite?

6

7

They're the most amazing gymnasts ever. Watch closely next time a kitty tiptoes along a fence or jumps from a high wall. Most can leap at least seven times their own body height.

8 They have the cutest little pink sandpaper tongues!

Cats have lots of ways of showing they're happy. As well as purring, they wind themselves around their owner's legs or start kneading with their paws.

9

10

Cats are very loyal. Some can even tell if their owners are happy, unwell, or sad.

did you know?

A group of cats is called a "clowder," but a clan of kittens is known as a "kindle."

Magical Markings

Every cat's a cutie. Find out about some of these eye-catching breeds, and then color the paw next to your favorite.

Birman

Creamy fur set off with dark points on its ears, face, legs, and tail. Snowy white feet and beautiful blue eyes.

Mixed breed

The most common kitten of all - each one is unique! Most of our pets are mixed breeds. Coats come in many colors - tabby, tortoise-shell, ginger, and more.

Siamese

Oriental puss that first came from Thailand. Slender body, almond-shaped eyes, and oversized ears. Prefers to live in pairs than alone.

Bengal

A wild-looking kitty that's really a softie! Leopardlike spots, rosettes and stripes on its body, with a lighter, fluffy tummy.

Persian

Long-haired fluffy cats that adore being stroked and groomed.

Scottish Fold

Adorable kitties with little creases in their ears, making them curl over like a cap. Large round eyes and face.

Super Senses

Not many creatures can outsmart the eyes and ears of a cat.
Are you tuned in to your kitty's super senses?
Take this quiz to find out!

1

Cats have scent glands on their paws. When they scratch, they leave a smell behind to mark their territory.

TRUE ☐

FALSE ☐

2

Cats are able to see clearly, even in complete darkness.

TRUE ☐

FALSE ☐

3

Cats can only see in black and white.

TRUE ☐

FALSE ☐

4

Cats have an amazing sense of hearing. They can pick up very high-pitched sounds.

TRUE ☐

FALSE ☐

5

Cats' eyes have an extra layer that reflects light and makes them glow in the dark.

TRUE ☐

FALSE ☐

TRUE ☐

FALSE ☐

6

Cats use their whiskers to bat off flies and mosquitoes that get too close.

TRUE ☐

FALSE ☐

7

As well as using their noses to sniff things out, cats have a scent organ in their mouths.

8

Cats have fewer taste buds than humans, and they are less able to pick up the taste of sweet, sugary foods.

FINISH

Check your answers on page 80.

TRUE ☐

FALSE ☐

did you know?

Do you suffer from ailurophilia? This is the dictionary term for someone who is fond of cats and kittens.

Secret Lives

What does your cat get up to when you're busy at school, playing outside, or fast asleep? Take a peek into this secret journal. A pussycat's schedule is a whole lot different to ours!

TIME	ACTIVITY
5:45 AM	Meow loudly until my owner wakes up.
7:30 AM	Breakfast.
8:30 AM	Playtime! Go crazy running around the house.
10:15 AM	Take a nap to recover.
MIDDAY	Still got some serious sleeping to do!
2:00 PM	Move to a sunnier spot to sleep a bit more.
3:30 PM	Rise and stretch!

TIME	ACTIVITY
4:00 PM	Puss pampering session.
5:30 PM	Dinnertime.
7:30 PM	Relax and watch TV with my owner.
10:00 PM	Owner goes to bed. Take catnap.
MIDNIGHT	Go outside.
2:30 AM	Visit next door neighbor's house. Polish off their cat food.
3:30 AM	Patrol the neighborhood. Bravely scare off an unwanted intruder.
5:15 AM	Sunrise. Early morning tree-climbing session.
5:30 AM	Go home to check on my owner.

Too Cute!

What can I say? The camera loves me!

CHAPTER 2

Smitten with Kittens

Goldfish are great, dogs are awesome, but kittens are truly irresistible! If you've always dreamed of caring for a kitten, or are even lucky enough to have one already, then this is the chapter for you.

What's in a Name?

Your cat is amazing, so it deserves an amazing name!
When you're trying to choose, you can let your imagination run
wild. These pages will help you think up something fabulous.
You could keep the name in mind for a real kitty or one that you
would love to have in the future.

Choose the word you like best from each panel. Put them
all together to create a sparkling new name!

Misty
Pumpkin
Buttons
Princess
Lady
Professor

1

2

Sheba
Toby
Precious
Cupcake
Charlie
Emerald

Mitzie
Tinkerbelle
Marshmallow
Midnight
Fritz
Whiskers

3

Cleopatra
Horace
Diamante
Starlight
Minette
Maurice

4

5

Fluffysocks
Snowflake
Peanut
Errol
Anastasia
Paddypaws

My perfect pussycat name is

Pedigree cats have long names that have to be officially recorded. The first part of the name is chosen by the breeder and used for all of their kittens, so that everyone can tell what family the cat comes from.

A Fluffy New Friend

Kittens are tiny and delicate. When you meet one, take care to approach it calmly and gently. Follow the advice on these pages, and you'll soon have a fluffy friend that loves to be stroked and pampered.

Pick me up!

Some kittens love being held, while others immediately want to get down. Always pick a puss up with both hands, taking care to support the kitten's back legs and tail. If it tries to wriggle free, put it down right away.

Make a fuss

When you stroke your kitten, smooth the hair down in the direction that it grows. Tickling gently under its chin with a finger will make it feel super-relaxed.

Tummy trouble?

Unlike pups, most kittens don't like their bellies being stroked. Cats are natural hunters, so lying on their backs can make them feel vulnerable. Most prefer to sit upright while they are being petted.

Ribbons and Trims

Once your kitten has got to know you, it will happily let you groom its fur. You might even want to try out some feline fashion! Follow these rules to make sure you and your cat are happy and safe.

Dress-up rules!

1 Ask an adult before you start. Choose a costume that allows your pet to move freely and go to the toilet if it needs to.

2 Check that your kitten can see and hear properly in its costume and that there are no parts that it could chew and swallow.

3 Don't put your pet in anything that will make it overheat.

4 Only keep your kitten dressed up for a short amount of time. Don't let it roam outside with clothes on, as it could get its outfit caught.

5 Reward your pet with lots of treats for being a star. If it doesn't seem comfortable, however, take the costume off right away.

Collar for a Cutie

These gorgeous kitties need new collars! Get some pens or pencils, and then design a cute collar for each puss. Don't forget to color them.

Choose names for the kittens, and write them in the frames.

Can I get this in an extra small?

Fancy Hats

Marmalade is going to his first-ever party. Can you help him get dressed up? Use felt-tip pens to decorate his party hat and bow tie, and then draw a balloon for him to hold.

Night Night Sleep Tight

Kittens need lots of naptime! You can buy a bed from a pet shop, but it's much more fun to make your own. When it comes to bedtime, kittens don't have expensive taste - all you need is an old cardboard box!

1 Find a cardboard box that's the right size to comfortably fit your kitten inside.

Not too small!

Not too big!

Just right!

Mine. Mine!

2 Allow your pet to come and check the box out. Let it look inside and smell the box, so that it gets used to it.

Top Tip!

If you don't yet have your own kitty, why not make a bed for a favorite toy or someone else's pet?

3 Close all the flaps so that the box is sealed. Draw a circle on the front that is big enough for your kitten to jump in and out of. Ask an adult to cut the circle out.

This will do nicely!

4 Put some old newspapers inside the box to keep it warm. Find a blanket or towel to lay on top. If your kitten hasn't slept on the blanket or towel before, it might want to check them out first.

Home sweet home!

5 Choose a cozy corner to put your kitten's bed in. Lay some newspapers on the floor, and then rest the box on top. Your deluxe V.I.P. kitten apartment is ready to move into!

Why not?

1 Decorate your kitten's house with crayons or pens?

2 Write your kitten's name in big letters above the door?

3 Build a cardboard box extension with lots more holes for it to peep through?

Too Cute!

Shh! I'm counting mice.

CHAPTER 3

Purr-fectly Pampered

Every day, a cat will carefully lick its body and wash its face, so that its fur stays in tip-top condition. Many adore being brushed and pampered, too. Graceful, elegant, and well-groomed cats are born fashionistas!

Fluffy and Fabulous

Want to make your special pet feel like the cat's whiskers? Treat it to a grooming session! All kitties need brushing, especially those with fluffy long hair. It really is as easy as one, two, three...

Step 1

Spread an old towel across your knees, and invite your kitten onto your lap for a cuddle. It's important to make it feel calm and relaxed before you start grooming.

Step 2

Gently brush your kitten's back, sweeping the brush in the direction that the fur grows. If there are any knots or tangles, undo them little by little so that the hair isn't pulled.

Step 3

Work your way all over your kitten's body and legs. When you get to the tail, make a parting down the middle. Carefully brush out the fur on either side. Avoid your kitten's belly unless you are certain that it likes it.

A Furry Favor

Every time your kitten licks its coat, it swallows lots of loose hairs. Swallowing too many can make it sick. Grooming thins out the old hairs for your pet, as well as getting rid of mud and dirt. It also stops your pet's fur from getting matted, especially if it is long.

Brush ban

Not all kittens like being groomed - in fact, some will make a dash for the door at the first sight of a brush! Introducing grooming while your kitty is still young can help, but if it doesn't work out, don't worry. Cats are very efficient cleaners. Your pet is trying to tell you that it's got it covered!

Bad Hair Day!

Feline Fashionistas

So what are the cool cats wearing this season?
Our roving fashion reporter has snapped the latest in kitty cat-ure!
Color the paw print next to the look that you like the best.

Sergio Snapper

Top catarazzi photographer!

Tiddles

It takes a confident kitty to
pull off knitwear. Tiddles has nailed it!

Missy

When it comes to statement
hats, Missy likes to think big!

Princess

Princess's hat and skirt
combo is sooo this season!

Felix

Felix shows that even harnesses can be glam!

Muffin

Style icon Muffin keeps her look sweet and simple.

Buddy

Kitties can't get enough of Buddy's jazzy bow tie and vest ensemble.

Whiskers

Whiskers models the latest in cat accessories - the bag-dress.

Sailor

Sailor shows that a beret and shirt can be sleek and stylish!

Bella

Bella's tutu is so on-trend!

It's a Bling Thing!

Some kittens like living the high life! Get your prettiest pens or pencils, and give these cuties some extra sparkle. Draw on twinkling accessories, ribbons, and diamonds - the more fabulous the better!

1 This little cat fancies a new hat. Can you draw one for her?

2 It's time to say it with flowers. Draw some pretty blossoms in this kitten's fur and some butterflies above her head.

Nearly all kittens are born with blue eyes. However, most of them change to their true color within 12 weeks.

3 Sketch a pretty bow for this kitten, and then color it.

4 Fashionable felines love to sparkle! Give this pet a shimmering tiara or collar.

Kitty Caution
These delightful doodles are just for fun. If you want to safely dress up a kitty, check out the rules on page 19.

Very Important Pussycats

Want to impress your puss with a special treat? This letter grid is bursting with ways to please your favorite kitten! Twelve words are hiding in the panel below. Can you find them?

P	A	K	I	D	S	N	O	B	B	I	R
C	K	S	E	N	E	C	R	Y	L	T	C
U	Q	W	E	H	L	T	R	C	S	N	H
S	F	P	J	A	D	V	W	O	H	A	M
H	V	I	T	V	D	M	P	L	U	M	S
I	C	N	S	D	U	H	R	L	O	E	T
O	Z	T	J	H	C	S	B	A	Q	T	I
N	R	A	K	T	B	B	A	R	N	A	U
Q	L	C	A	J	M	X	S	Z	K	G	C
N	B	R	U	S	H	G	K	D	G	Y	S
F	C	O	X	B	N	R	E	F	J	S	I
S	Q	U	E	A	K	Y	T	O	Y	P	B

SCRATCH POST	
COLLAR	
RIBBONS	
CATNIP	
NAME TAG	
BISCUITS	

| SQUEAKY TOY | | FISH | | CUDDLES | |
| BASKET | | CUSHION | | BRUSH | |

Check your answers on page 80.

did you know?

Catnip is a type of plant with purple flowers. Most kittens absolutely adore it! It makes some get playful and excited. while others lay back dreamily. taking in the plant's minty scent.

Too Cute!

Trust me, I'll grow into them!

CHAPTER 4

Playtime!

Chase, catch, or hide-and-seek - all kittens love to play! Cats are naturally curious animals that want to explore new things. It's not just for fun, either. Rough and tumble games keep your kitty fit, as well as teaching it how to hunt.

Winning by a Whisker

If a kitten spends a lot of time indoors, it will quickly get bored.
How claw-ful! Don't despair - here are five giggly games
to play with your feline friend.

Scrunch!

This game really is as simple as it sounds. Take
a piece of paper and scrunch it up loosely
into a ball. Your kitten will be fascinated by
the noise! Let your kitten chase and stalk the
paper, and then wait for it to rip it up with
its tiny teeth.

Hide-and-seek

Get your kitten's attention and make sure that
it's in the mood for a game. Let its eyes follow
you as you hide behind a sofa or under a
table. Your puss will start to track and then
stalk you all the way to your hiding spot!

Cat-and-mouse!

Find a stuffed mouse, squeaky toy, or ball.
Hold it loosely in your fingers, and then move
it quickly left and right. No kitten will be able
to resist playing chase!

Bag catch

Put a big paper bag in the middle of the floor. It won't take long for your kitten to climb inside it. As soon as it's inside, gently flick the outside of the bag with your fingers. Your pussycat will dart left and right, trying to catch the noise!

Yarn romp!

Loosely unravel a ball of wool, and invite your kitten to play. Your cat will roll and tumble, holding the ball in its paws and trying to bite it. Never let your kitten play this game on its own, however - it could get tied up or choke on the yarn.

Watch out for claws! Kittens can get rough when they are excited.

Top Tip!

Kittens are naughty and nice - watch their games closely to make sure they don't get into trouble!

Did you know?

When your cat walks, it leaves only a single line of footprints. As it moves, it places each hind paw almost exactly in the print of the front paw. This means that it can walk in a very precise line along a fence or the back of the sofa.

Gone Fishing

You don't need to buy expensive toys - it's easy to keep your pet entertained! Learn how to make a fishing pole that will turn your cute kitty into a hunter with cat-titude.

You will need

- Three or four colorful feathers
- String
- Small metal bell (optional)
- Scissors
- Mint dental floss
- A garden cane

1

Gather the feathers into a bunch, and ask an adult to help you tie them together. Wind string around and around the feathers, and then tie it in a knot.

Top Tip!

Before you knot the string, you could thread in a jingly metal bell.

Unwind at least 20 in. (50 cm) of mint-flavored dental floss. Tie one end to the bunch of feathers and the other end to the garden cane.

3

2

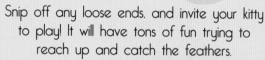

Snip off any loose ends, and invite your kitty to play! It will have tons of fun trying to reach up and catch the feathers.

WARNING:

Never leave your cat or kitten alone with the fishing pole. It could get caught in the line or chew a bit off the toy and swallow it.

How Old?

Cat Years	Human Years	Cat Years	Human Years
1	15	11	60
2	24	12	64
3	28	13	68
4	32	14	72
5	38	15	78
6	40	16	80
7	44	17	84
8	48	18	88
9	51	19	92
10	58	20	96

did you know?

Kittens and cats age at a different rate to us. Look at the chart to find out how old your pet is in human years.

Cats Do the Funniest Things

Cats are natural comedians! Read the animal gags, and then try them out on your family and friends.

What kinds of cats like bowling?

Alley cats!

What do you get if you cross a cat with Father Christmas?

Santa Claws!

What is a cat's favorite color?

Purr-ple!!

What do kittens eat for breakfast?

Mice Krispies!

Why did the kitten hide from the tree?

It was scared of the bark!

Why was the kitten so tiny?

It would only drink condensed milk!

What did the cat say when she lost her wallet?

I'm paw!

What do you call a cat that wears lipstick?

A glamor-puss!

What do you call a kitten with eight legs?

An octo-puss!

What is a cat's favorite TV show?

The Morning News!

What do you call a cat that's eaten a duck?

A duck-filled fatty-puss!

41

CHAPTER 5

Feline Feelings

Cats are very intelligent - they can understand a lot more than most people realize! Try talking to your cat - as well as helping you to bond, your pet will soon learn simple commands.

Meow!

Kittens talk all the time! To properly understand what they are saying, you need to look at the way they move their bodies and tails. Then, check off the moods that you've seen in your pet pal.

1

I'm having a good day!
Body check: walking happily, ears tilted forward, tail swaying gently.

2

I'm so pleased to see you!
Body check: head upturned, ears fully forward, tail pointing straight up.

3

Wanna be friends?
Body check: eyes interested, tail upright but curled at the end.

4

Mmm! I'm super-relaxed!
Body check: rolled onto back, tummy exposed, legs stretched out lazily.

I need to investigate!
Body check: head pointing down, ears focused forwards, tail lowered a little.

You're making me uneasy.
Body check: sitting or crouching, ears upright or forwards, tail swishing left and right.

Help! I'm scared.
Body check: back arched, fur starting to rise, tail tucked downwards.

You're making me angry!
Body check: back arched, ears pushed back, tail fluffed out and upright.

did you know?

Sometimes, kittens will show a mixture of these signs at the same time. When they play fight, cats pretend to be angry or fierce as part of the game.

Let's Talk!

It's important to talk to your cat when you're together. As well as helping you become friends, your pet will soon learn simple commands. Follow these tips for kitty chatting.

Chat to your cat!

 1 Decide on a few short commands and use them regularly. Always repeat the same words, so that your pet starts to recognize them. "Dinnertime," "bed!" and "down!" are all useful.

 2 Raise your voice when you're pleased with your puss so that she knows that she's been good.

 3 Talk quietly but firmly in a low voice when you want to tell your cat not to do something. A short sharp hissing sound sends it an instant message to stop!

Top Tip!

When you talk to your kitty, blink slowly
as you look at him or her. Usually it will
step closer to you. Slow, steady blinks make
it clear that you are a trusted friend.

Translating from cat

Short meow	Hi! Nice to see you!
Series of quick meows	Where have you been?
	I'm waiting for you!
Long, wailing meow	Feed me/let me outside now!
Low rumble or moan	Be warned – I don't like this!
Hiss	Stay away! I'm feeling scared or angry.
Purr	I am relaxed and so happy
	to be with you!

did you know?

Oriental breeds of cats, such as the Siamese and
Burmese, are great communicators. They use their
meowing to "talk" and convey all sorts of meanings.
Some are believed to make over 100 unique sounds.

47

Kitty Myths

Do our furry friends have a spooky sixth sense? Could they really have nine lives? There are so many myths about kitties!

Myth 1

Kittens always land on their feet...

Kitties are expert climbers that very rarely fall. When they do take a tumble from a height, they use a special self-righting reflex to twist around so that they land on their paws. No pet has super-powers, however, and sadly there are no guarantees that a puss can pull off a perfect landing every time.

Myth 2

Cats have nine lives...

Cats and kittens have sharp senses and quick wits. They don't have extra lives – they just seem to dodge danger more often than other animals can.

Myth 3

Well-loved kittens feast on fish for dinner...

Many pet-lovers think that they are treating their kitty by serving up a sardine or opening a can of tuna. Although many cats do like fish every now and then, they shouldn't eat too much of it. Cats are carnivores – they need the nutrients and vitamins in meat to stay healthy and strong.

Myth 4

All cats hate water...

Many kittens are actually fascinated by water, especially dripping faucets and showers! This myth isn't all nonsense, however. While a cat's coat has some water resistance, if it is completely submerged, the fur becomes waterlogged and heavy. Although there are always some swim-loving exceptions, most kittens don't like this sensation.

Myth 5

Black cats are lucky...

That all depends on where you happen to live! In Britain and Japan, a black cat crossing the street in front of you is thought to be a sign of good fortune. In the USA and several other countries, black cats are seen as bad omens, rooted in witchcraft. Of course, neither myth is true - black cats are just as gorgeous and lucky as any other color!

Myth 6

Cats have a sixth sense...

Cats and kittens don't have a special extra sense, but the five that they do have are super-effective. They are sensitive to the slightest of sounds and are even able to detect tiny vibrations. Because of this, a cat can sense Earth tremors and other dangers many minutes before its human owner can.

Too Cute!

It's not easy being an early learner.

CHAPTER 6

Cat Tails

When it comes to animal magic, kitties have always stood out from the crowd. People can't help falling for their elegance, charm, and claw-some good looks! Is there a superstar cat living in your house?

Superstar Cats

The movies, TV, and cartoon shows are full of cute kitties!
Can you identify the famous cats from the clues?

1 MOT

The original cartoon cat. He spends his days trying to get his claws into a mouse called Jerry.

OLMI

2

The cat that goes on an adventure with puppy pal, Otis.

ESJS

3

Postman Pat's devoted black-and-white cat.

RIHPADCL

4

Bob the Builder's curious blue puss.

NEBLWOLS

5

The scary kitty that Stuart Little meets when he moves to New York City.

FALGREDI

6

A cheeky comic book puss that lives with Odie the hapless dog.

TPO ACT

7

Yellow-furred alley cat that drives Officer Dibble crazy.

YERVSTLES

8

Tweety Bird drives this puddy tat crazy!

Check your answers on page 80.

Did you know?

Some cats are used to living the high life. In 1988, a cat called Blackie inherited millions of dollars from his owner, Ben Rea. The millionaire didn't leave a penny to his family, opting to give his money to animal charities instead.

Purring Pages

Next time you snuggle up in bed, take a book down from the shelf. Litter-ature is full of wonderful pussycat characters! Color the paw next to the ones you have read!

The Cheshire Cat

There is something very mysterious about the Cheshire Cat! He appears - and disappears - in Lewis Carroll's classic novel *Alice's Adventures in Wonderland*. The magical creature can fade away, leaving just its grin floating in the air.

Hermione's pet appears in J. K. Rowling's Harry Potter stories. He is a big ginger tom with a flat face. As well as being loyal and intelligent, Crookshanks is believed to be half-cat and half-kneazle.

Crookshanks

Gobbolino

Ursula Moray Williams' story was published back in 1942. Gobbolino is a little black kitten with a white paw and bright blue eyes. His sister, Sootica, can't wait to be a witch's cat, but Gobbolino yearns for a quiet life in a cozy kitchen.

Slinky Malinki

Slinky Malinki was dreamed up by Lynley Dodd. By day he is a common black stay-at-home cat. By night he transforms into an adventurer that prowls the neighborhood looking for trouble.

The Cat in the Hat

Who can forget the Cat in the Hat! Dr. Seuss's crazy creation wears a red-and-white striped top hat and a scarlet bow tie. He and his pals Thing One and Thing Two seem to have only one thing on their minds - trouble!

Tom Kitten

English storyteller Beatrix Potter painted little Tom Kitten over a hundred years ago. Tom is one of Tabitha Twitchit's three pussycat children. In the story, Tom, Mittens, and Moppet ruin a posh tea party by not doing what they're told.

Tabby McTat

Former Children's Laureate Julia Donaldson created this rhyming story with artist Axel Scheffler. Although he's a little scruffy, Tabby is an adorable busker's cat. His owner, Fred, loves him very much.

Cleopatra's Cats

Humans have shared a special bond with cats for thousands of years! It is believed that the first people to take the cat into their hearts and homes were the Ancient Egyptians. The rest, as they say, is hiss-tory!

Marvelous mousers

The Ancient Egyptians quickly realized that as well as being refined and dainty, cats could be useful, too. A tame kitten in the house was able to protect important food stores by hunting rats and mice.

Cats had other uses, too. As well as protecting their families from poisonous snakes, they were able to catch game. Cats were taken into the marshes along the Nile to hunt birds.

The lap of the gods

The Ancient Egyptians valued cats more than any other animals. They prayed to them and built temples in their honor. One of the most famous goddesses was called Bastet. Sculptures show her as a woman with a cat's head. Bastet was also known as "Pasht," which could be where our modern-day word "puss" comes from.

Special treatment

In the days of Cleopatra and the pharaohs, all cats had to be treated with respect. Many were dressed in gold necklaces and jewels. Even stray cats had fine food left out for them to eat. If you killed a cat, even accidentally, the punishment was death.

When a cat died, the whole family would go into mourning. As a mark of respect, both rich and poor people would shave off their eyebrows. The cat's body would be treated with oils, then sent to embalmers to be turned into a mummy.

The Egyptian Mau is a special breed that is said to look very like the cats that lived in the days of Ancient Egypt. Although some claim that the kitties might actually be descended from these exotic ancestors, this hasn't been proved.

did you know?

Nearly every ginger kitten born is a boy. Males are known as "tom cats."

My Cat Tail

Do you have a tale that you'd love to tell? Use this space to write your own kitten story. It could be true or imagined.

did you know?

Manx kittens are born without tails. They seem to get on just fine without them!

CHAPTER 7

It's a Pussycat's World!

Kittens are our most popular pets, paws-down!
There are all sorts of ways to tell the world that you're a cat
person. You can say it with posters, wear a kitty costume, or
hold a pussycat party for all of your friends!

Pussycat Party!

Have you ever had a joint birthday party... with your pet?
With a little planning and some clever kitty crafting, you could host
the purr-fect pussycat party!

Paws for thought...

Design your invites in the shape of
a cat paw. Use the template below
to trace around, then cut them out.
Don't forget to ask your guests to
dress up in cat tails, masks, and ears!

You are
INVITED
to
Caitlyn's
KITTY-STYLE PARTY
ON **September 10th**
AT **1 until 3**
R.S.V.P **Caitlyn**

You are
INVITED
to
_____
KITTY-STYLE PARTY

ON _____

AT _____

R.S.V.P _____

Cute collars

Instead of stickers, use ribbons to make adorable name "collars" to give to your guests when they arrive. Cut out a circle of card and hole punch a hole through the middle. Write a name on the card, and then thread the ribbon through the card. You could write your friends' real names or choose a cat name for each of them instead.

Decorations

Hang sweet kitten posters around the room, and then use a pen to decorate your balloons with cat faces and whiskers. Ask your friends to bring their cuddly toy cats to sit next to them at the party table.

Fishy food!

Ask a grown-up to trim tuna sandwiches into fish shapes, or serve up bowls of gummy fish candy. You could even mix frosted cereal and popcorn to make bowls of kibble!

Great Games

Theme your games to match the occasion. You could try pin the tail on the pussycat, hunt the mouse all around the house, or make a cat pinata - see below!

Kitty pinata

You will need

- Balloon
- Torn-up strips of newspaper
- Glue
- String
- Candy
- Adhesive tape
- Confetti (optional)
- Scissors
- Card
- Tissue paper
- Paints

1 Start by blowing up your balloon and tying it securely with a knot.

2 Then, using the glue and strips of torn newspaper, cover the balloon all over and leave it to dry.

3 Make a hole in the balloon and fill the shell with candy and confetti. Then, take the string and tape a loop inside the top.

4 Using more strips of the torn newspaper, cover the hole and leave to dry thoroughly.

5 Cut out some card ears and stick them onto the head. To finish, cover with tissue paper and paint on the cat's features. Now you can hit it!

Draw your cat face here first - don't forget
to add whiskers!

Calendar Kittens

Use this cute calendar to make every day purr-fect!
Circle the birthdays of all your family and friends.

JANUARY

1	2	3	4	5	6	7
8	9	10	11	12	13	14
15	16	17	18	19	20	21
22	23	24	25	26	27	28
29	30	31				

Snowflakes make kitty's
whiskers tickle!

FEBRUARY

1	2	3	4	5	6	7
8	9	10	11	12	13	14
15	16	17	18	19	20	21
22	23	24	25	26	27	28
29						

Will you be
my Valentine?

MARCH

1	2	3	4	5	6	7
8	9	10	11	12	13	14
15	16	17	18	19	20	21
22	23	24	25	26	27	28
29	30	31				

Spring kitty is
feeling pretty!

APRIL

1	2	3	4	5	6	7
8	9	10	11	12	13	14
15	16	17	18	19	20	21
22	23	24	25	26	27	28
29	30					

Every great journey starts
with one small step.

MAY

1	2	3	4	5	6	7
8	9	10	11	12	13	14
15	16	17	18	19	20	21
22	23	24	25	26	27	28
29	30	31				

May blossoms beautifully,
just like kitty!

JUNE

1	2	3	4	5	6	7
8	9	10	11	12	13	14
15	16	17	18	19	20	21
22	23	24	25	26	27	28
29	30					

When June comes, kitty can't
help thinking sweet things.

JULY

1	2	3	4	5	6	7
8	9	10	11	12	13	14
15	16	17	18	19	20	21
22	23	24	25	26	27	28
29	30	31				

School's out and summer's here - everybody cheer!

AUGUST

1	2	3	4	5	6	7
8	9	10	11	12	13	14
15	16	17	18	19	20	21
22	23	24	25	26	27	28
29	30	31				

Even kitties like to get away from it all!

SEPTEMBER

1	2	3	4	5	6	7
8	9	10	11	12	13	14
15	16	17	18	19	20	21
22	23	24	25	26	27	28
29	30					

It's getting cooler, let's cozy up!

OCTOBER

1	2	3	4	5	6	7
8	9	10	11	12	13	14
15	16	17	18	19	20	21
22	23	24	25	26	27	28
29	30	31				

Trick or treating anyone?

NOVEMBER

1	2	3	4	5	6	7
8	9	10	11	12	13	14
15	16	17	18	19	20	21
22	23	24	25	26	27	28
29	30					

Brrr... it's cold outside! Luckily, kitty loves to snuggle.

DECEMBER

1	2	3	4	5	6	7
8	9	10	11	12	13	14
15	16	17	18	19	20	21
22	23	24	25	26	27	28
29	30	31				

Have yourself a merry kitty Christmas!

did you know..?

Cats are the world's most popular pet.
There are three cats for every family dog.

Cool Cats

Are you an expert on all things fluffy, furry, and feline?
Take this test to find out!

1. How many meals a day do kittens need to eat?

A. six

B. one

C. three to four

D. two to three ✓

2. What animal are pet cats descended from?

A. lynx

B. African wildcat

C. Bengal tiger ✓

D. lion

3. What is the name of the toe that sits a little way up a kitten's leg on the inside?

A. dew claw

B. scratching claw

C. hind toe ✓

D. big toe

4. Which of these foods should never be given to a cat?

A. onions ✓

B. cheese

C. tuna

D. cooked meat

5. What breed of cat has no tail?

A. Siamese ☐

B. Manx ☑

C. Cornish Rex ☐

D. Birman ☐

6. How many baby teeth do kittens start out with?

A. 18 ☑

B. none ☐

C. 42 ☐

D. 26 ☐

7. Why do cats rub themselves against their owner's legs?

A. to show they're hungry ☐

B. to spread their scent ☑

C. to trip them up ☐

D. to say hello ☐

8. What type of plant drives kitties crazy?

A. catnip ☑

B. catkins ☐

C. daisies ☐

D. daffodils ☐

did you know?

Check your answers on page 80.

Calico kittens have fur that grows in patches of white, black, and orange. They are nearly always girls.

Too Cute!

So busted! Must. Act. Irresistible.

CHAPTER 8

Kittens 4 Ever

Big eyes, pointy tails, and soft paddy paws - what do pussycats mean to you? Use this chapter to write about the kitten you love the most, get arty, and then discover your own cat characteristics!

Pussycat Pals

This is your very own feline fact file! Write about your own special pet or the kitten you'd love to meet.

Name: Molly Pop

Boy or girl: girl

Age: 6 — 40

Fur color: Black & white

Eye color: Green

Put a picture of your pussycat pal here.

Unusual markings: ....

....

....

The things it does that make me laugh: Molly Makes me Laugh When she chases her tail.

....

....

....

Breed: ___ Short haires

Favorite toy: Stinky
Samon

Favorite food: chicken

Five words to describe my kitten:
1.
2.
3.
4.
5.

What makes my cat special: ....
....
....

Draw a picture of your pussycat pal here.

Pretty as a Picture

Could you be the next "Clawed" Monet? Drawing a cute kitten picture needn't be difficult, as long as you take it one step at a time...

You will need

- A pencil
- Eraser
- White paper
- Fine point black pen
- Pencil sharpener

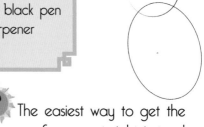

1 First, find your subject. It is much easier to draw a cat if you've got one to look at! (You could use a color photo of a kitty instead.) Sit with a sketchbook on your lap.

2 The easiest way to get the shape of your pet right is to draw a soft outline first. Look carefully at your kitten, and then draw an oval shape for its body, and a circle for its head. The circle should overlap the oval slightly.

3 Draw in two legs, starting at the point where the kitten's head meets its body. Add two rounded back legs at the sides.

4 Sketch the curve of a tail coming around on one side. This might be big and bushy or thin and sleek. Look carefully at your cat subject. Add some ears to your cat's head. Are they big or small?

5 Now gently erase the circles and lines that you drew at the start. You should be left with a perfect cat outline.

6 Carefully draw in the kitten's features. Add two almond-shaped eyes that sit above the nose and whisker area.

7 Use your pencil to carefully shade in the kitten's coat. Brush each pencil stroke in the same direction so that it looks like real fur. Build up with different shades to make your portrait as realistic as possible.

8 Your portrait is almost there! Use the fine point pen to add some definition to the picture. Highlight the eyes, add detail, and draw in fine strokes for whiskers.

did you know?

Famous painters Matisse, Picasso, and Salvador Dali all loved cats!

Fur Real!

Curious, elegant, and playful – maybe cats aren't so different from us after all? Take this quiz to find out what kitten qualities you share with your pet!

1. Your favorite weekend is spent...

A. exploring somewhere new ☐

B. playing in the park ☐

C. chilling out with my family ☐

D. shopping with friends ☑

2. Most of the time, your bedroom is...

A. full of books and mags ☐

B. a complete mess ☐

C. cozy and warm ☑

D. littered with clothes ☐

3. Your best birthday gift would be...

A. a digital camera ☐

B. a trampoline ☐

C. a cuddly cat toy ☑

D. a cute pair of shoes ☐

4. Your favorite item of clothing is...

A. your sneakers ☐

B. your comfiest jeans ☐

C. your PJs ☐

D. your princess tiara ☑

5. When your friends come over, you love to...

- A. go rollerblading ✓
- B. play hide-and-seek
- C. snuggle up with a movie ✓
- D. give each other makeovers ✓

6. Your favorite subject at school is...

- A. science
- B. gym
- C. English
- D. art ✓

Mostly As - curious kitty

You're a classic cat person - curious, quick-witted, and intelligent! You like to follow your nose and find out new things.

Mostly Bs - playtime pussycat

You're up for fun and always have time for a game. No wonder everybody loves to be around you!

Mostly Cs - cuddly cat

Laid-back, dreamy, and affectionate sums you up purr-fectly! You're a home cat who stays loyal to family and friends.

Mostly Ds - fabulous feline

You're elegant, graceful, and creative. People and pussycats adore the way you can make any day furr-bulous!

Utterly lovable!

Look at the photos, and then write a funny caption underneath each one. The first one has been filled in to get you started...

I'm a big scary monster, aarr!

Can you get me down?

Cute cozy and cozy.

Just chillin.

Cats rarely meow at other cats. They tend to just meow at humans!

Iz yntes this

one cool cat

I ruv U

just Hangih

Answers

Pages 10-11
Super Senses
1. True
2. False - cats can't see in total darkness, but they can see much better in low light than humans and many other animals can.
3. False - they can see in color, but not in the same way that we do. Some colors look less intense in cat vision.
4. True - in fact, they can even hear higher sounds than dogs can.
5. True
6. False - whiskers are very sensitive. Cats use them to sense obstacles and hunt for food.
7. True
8. True

Pages 32-33
V.I.P.s! (Very Important Pussycats)

P	A	K	I	D	S	N	O	B	B	I	R
C	K	S	E	N	E	C	R	Y	L	T	C
U	Q	W	E	H	L	T	R	C	S	N	H
S	F	P	J	A	D	V	W	O	H	A	M
H	V	T	V	D	M	P	L	U	M	S
	C	N	S	D	U	R	L	O	E	T
O	Z	T	J	H	C	S	B	A	Q	T
N	R	A	K	T	B	B	A	R	N	A	U
Q	L	C	A	J	M	X	S	Z	K	G	C
N	B	R	U	S	H	G	K	D	G	Y	S
F	C	O	X	B	N	R	E	F	J	S	I
S	Q	U	E	A	K	Y	T	O	Y	P	B

Pages 52-53
Superstar Cats!
1. TOM
2. MILO
3. JESS
4. PILCHARD
5. SNOWBELL
6. GARFIELD
7. TOP CAT
8. SYLVESTER

Pages 68-69
Cool Cats Quiz
1. C
2. B
3. A
4. A
5. B
6. D
7. B
8. A

THE END
BYE!